Learning to Read, Step by Step!

Ready to Read   Preschool–Kindergarten
• big type and easy words • rhyme and rhythm • picture clues
For children who know the alphabet and are eager to begin reading.

Reading with Help   Preschool–Grade 1
• basic vocabulary • short sentences • simple stories
For children who recognize familiar words and sound out new words with help.

Reading on Your Own   Grades 1–3
• engaging characters • easy-to-follow plots • popular topics
For children who are ready to read on their own.

Reading Paragraphs   Grades 2–3
• challenging vocabulary • short paragraphs • exciting stories
For newly independent readers who read simple sentences with confidence.

Ready for Chapters   Grades 2–4
• chapters • longer paragraphs • full-color art
For children who want to take the plunge into chapter books but still like colorful pictures.

STEP INTO READING® is designed to give every child a successful reading experience. The grade levels are only guides; children will progress through the steps at their own speed, developing confidence in their reading.

Remember, a lifetime love of reading starts with a single step!

*The authors would like to thank Kaitlin Dupuis,
Deanna Ellis, and Darren Ward for their help
in creating this book.*

Text copyright © 2020 by Kratt Brothers Company Ltd.

Wild Kratts® © 2020 Kratt Brothers Company Ltd. / 9 Story Media Group Inc. Wild Kratts®,
Creature Power® and associated characters, trademarks, and design elements are owned by
Kratt Brothers Company Ltd. Licensed by Kratt Brothers Company Ltd.

Visit us on the Web!
StepIntoReading.com
rhcbooks.com

Educators and librarians, for a variety of teaching tools, visit us at
RHTeachersLibrarians.com

ISBN 978-1-9848-5111-6 (trade) — ISBN 978-1-9848-5112-3 (lib. bdg.) —
ISBN 978-1-9848-5113-0 (ebook)

Printed in the United States of America
10 9 8 7 6 5 4 3 2 1

WILD DOGS AND CANINES!

by Martin Kratt and Chris Kratt

Random House 🏠 New York

What is found all over
the world in different habitats?
What hunts together
in pairs or packs?
Canids!

Canids are a group of animals that includes canines such as wolves and coyotes.

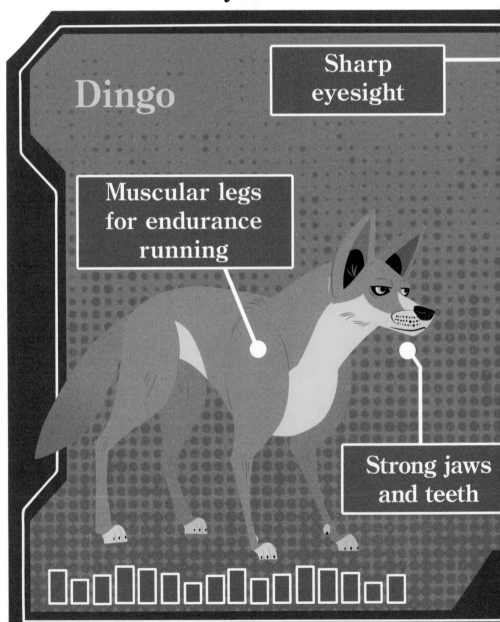

Dingo

Sharp eyesight

Muscular legs for endurance running

Strong jaws and teeth

The group also includes vulpines such as foxes. They all have many features in common.

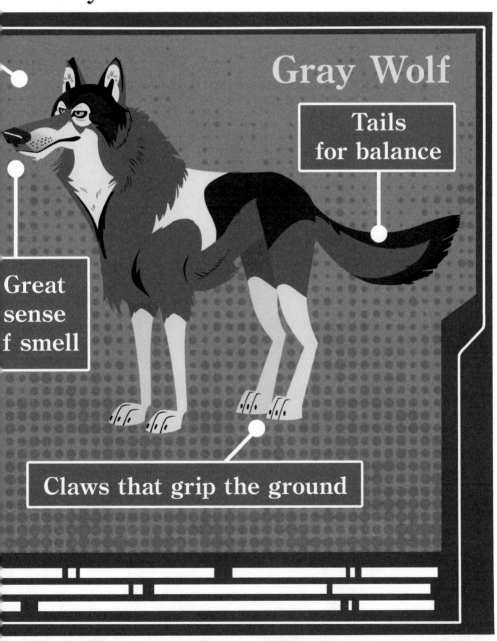

Gray Wolf

Tails for balance

Great sense f smell

Claws that grip the ground

There are about 36 different species of wild canids in the world.

"They come in many
different sizes," Chris says.
Martin suggests,
"Let's meet some of them!"

Fennec Fox

Fennec foxes are
the smallest canids!
They live in one of the world's
biggest deserts—the Sahara!

They don't have to
drink a lot of water.
They get water from
the food they eat.

Bat-Eared Fox

Another little big-eared fox

is the bat-eared fox.

They listen for insects to eat.

Then they lick beetles and termites right off the ground. SLURP!

Yum . . . termites!

Bush Dog

The South American bush dog is rarely seen. It can live in burrows or hollow tree trunks deep in the Amazon rain forest.

These tough dogs
share territory with
bigger predators
such as the jaguar!

Red Fox

These foxes live all around
the northern half of the world.
They can use their tail
to keep warm in cold weather.

Red foxes aren't always red!

They also come

in different colors,

like black or silver.

Dhole

The dhole is also called

the Indian wild dog.

Dholes are strong and fierce,

but they also work together.

A dhole pack can have 30 dogs!

Together, dholes
even take on
big predators,
such as tigers!

Coyote

The coyote is
a medium-sized canid.
Coyotes are very smart.
They eat all kinds of foods
and live in all kinds of habitats.

They survive in hot deserts, snow-covered prairies, tropical rain forests, and even cities!

African Wild Dog

African wild dogs are
also called painted dogs
because each one has
a unique coat pattern.

They hunt by chasing prey
across the savannah.
While the pack hunts,
one adult always stays at
the den to take care of the pups.

Uh-oh.
Today is
my turn!

Dingo

Dingoes live in Australia.
They can hunt alone
or in packs.

They hunt both
big and small prey,
from kangaroos
to rodents!

Hop to it!

Maned Wolf

Maned wolves have
very long legs so they can
see above the tall grass
of their South American home.

Ethiopian Wolf

This is one of the rarest canids.

These wolves survive in

the mountains of Ethiopia

and eat mostly giant mole rats.

Arctic Wolf

Arctic wolves are white
and blend into the snow.
They eat small creatures,
such as mice and lemmings.

Keep running,
wolf pack!

But they also use teamwork

to hunt bigger prey,

such as musk oxen.

Gray Wolf

Gray wolves work together as a pack when hunting prey or defending territory.

They use smells, body language, and sounds—like their famous howl—to communicate. A wolf pup starts to howl when it is only eight weeks old.

Foxes, wild dogs, coyotes, and wolves all have amazing Creature Powers!

We love them running free . . .

. . . and in the wild!